# Songs of the Three: Rhymes and songs from the Lunar series universe



Whittney Corum

BookLeaf Publishing
India | USA | UK

Songs of the Three: Rhymes and songs from the Lunar series universe © 2022 Whittney Corum



Presentation by *BookLeaf Publishing*

Web: www.bookleafpub.com

E-mail: info@bookleafpub.com

ISBN: 978-93-5744-977-9

First edition 2022

# DEDICATION

To my sisters, who are always beside me.

# ACKNOWLEDGEMENT

Thank you, my family, for supporting me in this.

# PREFACE

Welcome to the world of Kardian, in this book you will find rhymes and songs that will tell stories of the world. You will see the courtship of the Lady of Lace and Flickron and the birth of Elves and Humans. Please enjoy.

# Birth of Elves

Come to me, my children; it's time to hear
a story that we all hold dear,
for it is time for you to understand how we came
to this forest land.

X

You see once long ago,
The two sky sisters looked to the ground below.
The world was filled with their sister's creatures,
those of four feet and those of feathered feature.
So the Sun told her sister in the sky,
why don't we create something for our side.
The Lady of Lace, who was weaving at the time,
looked up from her twine.
She told her sister her voice laid with severe
thought.
What creature would I make that our sister has
not?
The Sun smiled and grabbed some dirt.
This is how I will do my work,
I will create a man from the ground,
like our father, but earthbound.
They will worship my light
and be guided by my might.
It was the then our Lady of Lace's turn;
she stood up and looked to the stars that burned.

I will use the lights of the sky and
take them and make them become mine.
They will be creatures of the night,
They will know wrong from right, and they will
live as long as a star,
they will be the ones whose eyes could see far,
They are the ones who will be forest's aids,
My children, the Elves, will be their name.
And that my child is the story of us.
We were created from stardust,
The lady of Lace, the oldest of the three,
has given birth to all the elves you see.

# Time to sleep (Elvish lullaby)

Hush now, little one, time to sleep.
The Lady Lace has started to weave.
Listen now, sleep sweet one, you will wake when the sun comes,
sleep you now, and dream of delight,
It will be alright,
Hush now, little one, time to sleep,
no more fears, no time to weep,
for it's time for you to sleep.
Hush, little one, I'm right here,
hush little one, I will make it clear,
you are the one I adore,
you are the one who needs more.
Hush now, little one, time to sleep,
the Lady of Lace will weave you a dream.

# Until Dawn (Elvish Lullaby)

Once in a lifetime, I found my way.

To the place of wonder,

of light and shade,

and there stood the lady dress in white,

ready for me shining the light.

She whispered to me I am here,

to guide you to dreams away from your fears,

and I was feeling so calm, I stay asleep until the dawn.

So when you sleep you hear her song, it will take you away until the dawn.

It will take you away until dawn.

# Wedding of Flickron and the Lady of Lace

Come, my children, and it's time to hear
a story that we all hold dear,
The story of love that stopped a war,
between the men of the North and us.

□

It was in days long past,
when the first elfin king rein was to pass
To his eldest son,
the elfin prince Orion,
They came from the North swords in hand,
their feet stained with the Bone Cliff's sand.
The ones who came from the Sky Father,
they came with his sons and daughters.
That's when the sister's three,
Came together by the Oaktree.
They deiced to fight,
to protect their people and light,
Yet as years passed,
and each breath became a person's last,
The three sisters and Father Sky,

came together to speak of life,
If the war was to end,
one sister would have to mend,
by wedding the youngest of the Northern men.
The Lady of Lace, her head held high
Took and breath and told Father Sky,
I will pay for the war,
I will marry your man from the North.
Sky Father nodded and called for the man,
the one who held a ball in his hand,
This is Flickron, my youngest son.
He shall be your promised one,
The youth was a strange sight to see,
his hair white blowing in the breeze,
his eyes gold like a fox
his hand and fingers ready to pick locks,
The Lady of Lace knew right away,
her promise one was the one that tricksters and thieves obey.
Yet, as she took his hand,
She felt safe and that she could stand,
With this god of tricks
who's fingers were dancing betwixt
her hand and wrist,
would be the one who she would tarry,
she would gladly marry,
to end the war
that took so many,
She would marry this God of Tricks,

be his bride to fix
the bridge between two people were now
intertwined
as the Lady of Lace and Flickron
became wrapped in a ball of twine.

# Praise for Solara

Solara, the daughter of Sky and Earth
hear the chant of your people
the creator of humans from the earth
we call on you on the day of Mila
to bless our land with your light
We call you to guide us this year and give us blessings
Solara, the daughter of Sky and Earth
We are all here to come forth
To see the rays of your power
we all come to know the intensity of light,
to help our crops grow
To use your light to guide us through the day.
Solara, The daughter of Sky and Earth
We humbly come to show our worth.

# Breath of Summer

Once in wintergreen, the lady came.

The sun is hidden from us for days to see her people in snow

Her voice filled the air like a breath of spring that was long gone.

I watched as she walked through the snow,

A yellow fire in the winter is white.

I came to her, watching as her sky blue eyes reflected the sun that she was named for.

I watched as she touched brought green to the dead trees, her warmth giving them strength.

She then looked at me, and I could see the summer coming. She then whispered to me like a swift wind.

"Be ready, for soon this world will be warm for the summer."

I nodded as she left again, disappearing into the winter wind.

# Dance of Solara (a dancing game)

Come see the butterflies dance around the roses there,

it is time to play the king's dare,
listen now and listen well,
Do what the king has to tell.
From high to low, over and under,
follow the kings order,
if you don't the game is over.

# Another Rhyme (Human song)

Mother Sun look down below,
Play the game that dances like so,
turn left, then right, reach up high, and grab the light.
Get on the floor, pick some flowers, and through them up to take showers.
Take your partner's hand and head off to a different land.

# Call of the Wild

The wild call my heart
the queen dressed n emerald sings,
A song of nature.

# Faia's love

The king of Shadow
love of nature beckons him
to Fania Queen Earth

# Aiden's Lullaby (From Mix Blood)

Child of wind and sea, child of earth and fire,
the child that belongs to me, a sweetheart desire.
Hear my song and sleep.
The Lady Lace gives you dreams, and your heart gives you wings.
Child of sun and moon, hear my happy tune.
Time has come to sleep, and in your dreams will keep.
Child of mine sweet dreams, sweet as the moonbeams.

# The one I love (From Mix Blood)

Across the sky,
the moon flies,
Across the stream, the bird sings,
across the dived is my love, and I will find a way to their side.
For I know a way to be there, I know a way to care, I know my heart.
And it doesn't want to part.
The sea and sky hear my cries and take my voice to the one.
The one who keeps my heart as warm as the sun.
The moon knows my feelings, she has sung the song before.
She knows I'm willing to find an open door. So I will be there to see the one I wish, I will be there to give the lovers kiss.

# The Lovers

Listen to me, children,
for the story, I'm about to tell,
will you dream of plenty and will make you
sleep well,
It happened when the snow fell,
that our lady moon was awake,
she was out a-hunting, looking for game to take,
While awhile a walking she came to spy,
a youth sleeping during this could night,
she swiftly went to him to see if would wake,
for she was worried that he was for death to
take,
to her surprise, as she touched him he woke,
his green eyes meeting her eyes of gray as stone,
"Who are ye, laying her in the winter night, are
you not afraid of death's bite?"
the youth answered after licking his lips,
"No, for death cannot touch me, for I have a
right, to find the lady of the moon and make her
my wife."
to this, the Lady Moon laughed for she knew
what the youth said was a fib,
"That cannot be because I'm promised to the
trickster Flickron."

"Then you are mine lady of the moon." the youth said,
As his hair changed from red,
Now standing was a man with silver hair on his head,
He had a smile which set the Lady Moon's heart aflame,
For she thought that he had been slain,
She held him tight and said his name,
He seemed to know her woes and pulled her close,
"Do not be sad my love, for I have passed all thy sisters' tests,
Their champions laid to rest. I came to the forest knowing that you'll be coming tonight and hunting for game so now I can give you my name."
Then he took her hand and whispered her name before saying,
"So now my love we must fly to your castle as my bride."
And so my children this is the end, for the Lady Moon is coming in,
it's for sleep to begin.

# The Story of Winter Fell

Come now, child, and listen well,
To the story of Winter Fell,
Where many warriors came to fight,
Yet most lost their life,
To protect their kingdom from the darkness of night,
They chose to take on the dragon's might,
To earn the princess as a bride,
And to earn the kingdom's pride,
Many lords and knights tried and failed,
to kill the dragon of the Fell,
Yet it was peasant son
Who went to face the dark one,
He took a sword and a shield and wished his parents well,
For he knew that if one faces the dragon of Fell,
that he might save his life as well,
Though before he left his home,
his mother gave him a magic spell,
That would protect him from the dragon's flame
So the peasant took the path to the dragon lair,
the wind flowing through his blond hair,

when he entered the dragon's home,
filled with burnt flesh and bone,
he took heart and stepped inside,
to face the dragon and win his bride,
Then comes the dragon breathing his flame,
He cares not what the boy is named
His jaws looking for human flesh
But the peasant was luckier than the rest
his mother charm is what saves his hide
for when the jaws of the dragon opened wide,
they were stopped from piercing his side,
by the magic spell which kept him alive,
this caused the dragon to be confused,
for he did not see the peasant bruised,
this came the peasant time to strike the monster hide,
the sword struck home through the dragon's bone,
right to the dragon's heart,
when that happened, the dragon tore apart,
Then what was left was a crystal heart,
which the peasant took it and gave it to the king,
who then put it in the ring of his bride to be,
and the peasant with glee in his heart,
took the princess with open arms,
lived with joyous delight in the castle for all to see,
so that my sweet children be,

the story of Winter Fell, and how our kingdom came to be.

# Someone like the Lady Lace (Shifter-drinking song)

Oh oh hay, the work is done today,
come to drink and play,
I hope Flickron is away,
we have gotten our work, and now we need rest,
we have seen it all we want the best,
we are lions, foxes, and wolves,
Eagles, bears, and sometimes fools,
bless by the trickster to change our shape,
we pray we find someone like the Lady of Lace
to take.
We love to drink, and to have fun,
the pretty women come to run,
they dance and sing and call us honey
we have love aplenty.
we saw it all we want the best,
we are lions, foxes, and wolves,
Eagles, bears, and sometimes fools,
bless by the trickster to change our shape,

we pray we find someone like the Lady of Lace
to take.
We pray we find some like the Lady of Lace to
take.

# Solara's prayer

My people come and look at my beauty. Let my light show you the way. I will guide you with my light, both night and day.

# Faia's Prayer

I pray that you hear
The call of the wild near,
That you love nature

# Lady of Lace's Prayer

Listen, children that I hold dear,
I pray that you do not fear,
that you treat others with a loving ear,
That you will treat others not higher or lower
than you,
that you will always be true,
that is my prayer for you.

www.ingramcontent.com/pod-product-compliance
Lightning Source LLC
Chambersburg PA
CBHW051755130826
49812CB00033B/1160
*9789357449779*